Guelph Public Library

J914.731 FEH
Fehlen, Douglas J., author.
Explore Moscow

AUG - - 2020

EXPLORE MOSCOW

by Douglas J. Fehlen

12 STORY LIBRARY
MORE TO EXPLORE

J914.731
FEH

www.12StoryLibrary.com

Copyright © 2020 by 12-Story Library, Mankato, MN 56002. All rights reserved. No part of this book may be reproduced or utilized in any form or by any means without written permission from the publisher.

12-Story Library is an imprint of Bookstaves.

Photographs ©: Polina Shestakova/Shutterstock.com, cover, 1; Sergey Dzyuba/Shutterstock.com, 4; Baturina Yuliya/Shutterstock.com, 5; Everett Historical/Shutterstock.com, 6; Martynova Anna/Shutterstock.com, 8; Sweetland Studio/Shutterstock.com, 9; Viacheslav Lopatin/Shutterstock.com, 10; Dmitrii Iarusov/Shutterstock.com, 11; Boris Stroujko/Shutterstock.com, 12; E. O./Shutterstock.com, 12; Baturina Yuliya/Shutterstock.com, 13; Yuriy Stankevich/Shutterstock.com, 14; one photo/Shutterstock.com, 15; Nikita_Maru/Shutterstock.com, 15; dimbar76/Shutterstock.com, 16; Sergey Petrov/Shutterstock.com, 16; Gubin Yury/Shutterstock.com, 17; Pavel L Photo and Video/Shutterstock.com, 18; A.Savin/FAL1.3, 19; Gints Ivuskans/Shutterstock.com, 19; EugeniaSt/Shutterstock.com, 20; Olgysha/Shutterstock.com, 21; Lunov Mykola/Shutterstock.com, 22; Anton Gvozdikov/Shutterstock.com, 23; Tykhanskyi Viacheslav/Shutterstock.com, 24; Dmitrii Iarusov/Shutterstock.com, 24; alexeyart1/Shutterstock.com, 25; hurricanehank/Shutterstock.com, 26; Alexey Broslavets/Shutterstock.com, 27; Anton Gvozdikov/Shutterstock.com, 27; Vladimir Mulder/Shutterstock.com, 28; seeyah panwan/Shutterstock.com, 29; Baturina Yuliya/Shutterstock.com, 30

ISBN
9781632357274 (hardcover)
9781632358363 (paperback)
9781645820147 (ebook)

Library of Congress Control Number: 2019938651

Printed in the United States of America
September 2019

About the Cover
Christ the Savior Cathedral in Moscow.

Access free, up-to-date content on this topic plus a full digital version of this book. Scan the QR code on page 31 or use your school's login at 12StoryLibrary.com.

Table of Contents

Moscow Is the Capital of the World's Largest Country 4

The City Is Nearly 900 Years Old 6

Russia's Capital Is the Face of the Nation 8

Moscow Drives the National Economy 10

World-Famous Buildings Make Up the Skyline 12

Moscow's Infrastructure Is Vast and Crowded 14

The City Is a Center for Russia's Arts Scene 16

Sports Are a Big Part of Moscow Life 18

Dramatic Views and Urban Adventures 20

A Destination City for Food and Shopping 22

Wealthy and Poor Live Differently 24

Moscow Knows How to Celebrate 26

Fun Facts about Moscow 28

Where in the World? 29

Glossary 30

Read More 31

Index 32

About the Author 32

1 Moscow Is the Capital of the World's Largest Country

Moscow is the largest city in Russia. It is one of the largest cities in Europe by area. Moscow is the capital of the biggest country in the world. Russia covers 6.6 million square miles (17 million sq km). It stretches almost halfway around the planet.

The city of Moscow covers 970 square miles (2,511 sq km). It wasn't always that large. Until 2012, it was 420 square miles (1,091 sq km). That year, Russian officials more than doubled the size of the city. They hope this will help ease overcrowding and traffic jams.

Moscow is in the west of Russia. The Moscow River winds through it. Many famous landmarks rise along the river's banks. The Kremlin is one. This group of buildings houses the Russian government.

Moscow is mostly flat. It is set on a large plain. But parts of the city are built on small hills. Moscow's highest point is in the southwest.

Many famous landmarks are built along the Moscow River.

The Sparrow Hills rise 830 feet (250 m) above sea level.

Russia is known for cold winters. But Moscow's weather is relatively mild. Winds carry warm air from the Atlantic Ocean. High temperatures average between 19 and 29 degrees Fahrenheit (-7.2 to -1.73°C) between November and March. This is warmer than other Russian cities. Summer days are usually comfortable, but temps can reach 100 degrees Fahrenheit (38°C).

Moscow receives about 23 inches (580 mm) of precipitation each year. Much of it falls as rain. Snow falls during the winter months.

312
Length in miles (502 km) of the Moscow River

- Within Moscow, dozens of bridges offer river crossings.
- The river provides drinking water to people in the city.
- It later flows into the Volga, Europe's longest river.

THINK ABOUT IT

Moscow is on an important Russian river. Why might people have decided to settle there? What are some advantages of being on a major waterway?

2

The City Is Nearly 900 Years Old

The first historical record of Moscow dates from 1147 CE. Moscow was not a city then. It was a small town. A prince named Yury Dolgoruky visited. His son later built a fort at the site. But it would be hundreds of years before Moscow became an important city.

Moscow's location on a major river helped. By 1500, Ivan the Great had united Russian lands around the city. Moscow served as Russia's capital until 1712.

Then Peter the Great moved the capital 400 miles (640 km) north to St. Petersburg.

Moscow regained capital status after the Russian Revolution. This struggle began in 1917. People called the Bolsheviks took power. They were led by a man named Vladimir Lenin. The revolution ended centuries of rule by tsars. It led to the formation of the Soviet Union.

During the Soviet era, Moscow was the seat of communist power.

Soldiers gather to take an oath of allegiance at the start of the Russian Revolution in 1917.

34
Number of Moscow princes, tsars, and empresses before the Russian Revolution

- Eight men served as leaders of the Soviet Union.
- Boris Yeltsin became the first post-Soviet president in 1992.
- Vladimir Putin took control of the government in 2000. After one term by Dmitry Medvedev, Putin regained the presidency in 2012.

Its rule extended to more than a dozen socialist republics. The nation's wealth was mostly owned and controlled by the government. Leaders in Moscow created five-year plans to guide the Soviet Union's economy.

Things were much different by the end of the twentieth century. Changes made by Mikhail Gorbachev led to the Soviet Union's collapse. The Russian Federation replaced it in 1992. Moscow remained the capital.

TIMELINE

1147: First mention of Moscow in historical texts.

1462: Ivan the Great takes power and expands Russian lands.

1533: Ivan the Terrible becomes the first tsar of Russia.

1755: Moscow University is founded. It is the first university in Russia.

1812: Napoleon invades, but Russian forces push back his French army.

1905: Muscovites fighting for better living conditions are defeated in the Revolution of 1905.

1917: Tsarist rule ends with the Russian Revolution.

1918: A communist system of Russian government is set up in Moscow.

1991: The Soviet Union collapses under political and economic pressures.

1992: Boris Yeltsin's presidential win starts a new era of Russian government.

Russia's Capital Is the Face of the Nation

More than 12 million people live in Moscow. This is more than twice as many as St. Petersburg, Russia's next largest city. Including the suburbs, Moscow's population exceeds 20 million. The city is growing rapidly, even as Russia's overall population shrinks.

Most Muscovites are of Russian heritage. Less than 10 percent of the people are of other ethnicities. The largest groups are Ukrainians, Tatars, and Armenians. Many people from these backgrounds are migrant workers.

There is a wide gap between rich and poor in Moscow. Wealthy people often own multiple homes and enjoy city entertainments. Meanwhile, many others live paycheck to paycheck.

The majority of people in Moscow are Christians. But there are other religious groups. Up to 2 million Muslims worship in city mosques. Moscow synagogues serve an estimated 500,000 Jews. And tens of thousands of Buddhists attend temple services.

Nearly all adults in Moscow can read and write. A strong school system helps make the city an important education center for Russia.

> Education is important in Moscow, where women outnumber men.

WOMEN OUTNUMBER MEN

Moscow has more women than men. This is also true of Russia as a nation. Experts point to different reasons. One is that many Soviet men died in World War II. A more modern explanation is that women live longer than men. Research says women recently born in Russia will live 11.4 years longer than their male peers.

2 million
Approximate number of students in Moscow in 2017

- More than 200,000 professionals are employed in education.
- City programs have been put in place to give all children access to a quality education.
- Teacher pay is connected to class size and students' academic performance.

4

Moscow Drives the National Economy

The Moscow International Business Center is a modern high-rise office district for financial and IT companies.

Moscow is the financial center of Russia. It contains much of the country's wealth. The average person earns a monthly salary of nearly 81,000 rubles ($1,234). That is almost double the Russian national average of 43,400 rubles ($660).

Many Muscovites work in manufacturing. They make food products, chemicals, machines, and other goods. The energy industry also employs many people. The city exports a lot of oil and natural gas. Moscow has more white-collar jobs than any other Russian city. Many of these jobs are in financial services and software development.

The economy of Moscow has changed in recent decades. The government once controlled most financial activity. But today Moscow's economy is closer to a market economy. The fall of the Soviet Union

WOMEN EARN LESS THAN MEN

Imagine being a hard-working woman in Russia. But you don't earn as much as a coworker with similar duties. The only difference: Your coworker is a man. This is common in Moscow. Women make three-quarters of the pay males do nationally. The good news? The pay gap is getting smaller. Moscow women have greater pay equity than other women in Russia.

69
Number of billionaires living in Moscow in 2018

- In 2017, Russia had the world's biggest gap between rich and poor.
- Between 2015 and 2016, the average Russian became 14 percent poorer.
- Moscow is a center of wealth inequality.

led to more private companies being allowed to do business.

The government still influences some economic areas. These include banking, oil, and gas. But individuals own many companies in the city. A super-rich class of business owners has emerged. These people are known as oligarchs. Wealth brings them great power and political influence. Today, it is estimated that 111 people control almost 20 percent of Russia's wealth.

Women earn only three-quarters of the pay men earn in Moscow.

5 World-Famous Buildings Make Up the Skyline

Moscow has buildings that are known around the world. Many are hundreds of years old. They help tell the story of the city. They also show the history of the Russian state.

There is no greater example than the Kremlin. It has housed Russia's government for centuries. The triangular fort's walls and towers were built in the fourteenth century. More than 20 buildings are inside. They include famous palaces and cathedrals.

The Grand Kremlin Palace was built in the nineteenth century. The building was home to Russia's last tsars. Today tourists marvel at its white walls and green roof along the Moscow River. The State Kremlin Palace was built more recently. Finished in 1961, the concrete and glass building held Communist Party events for decades.

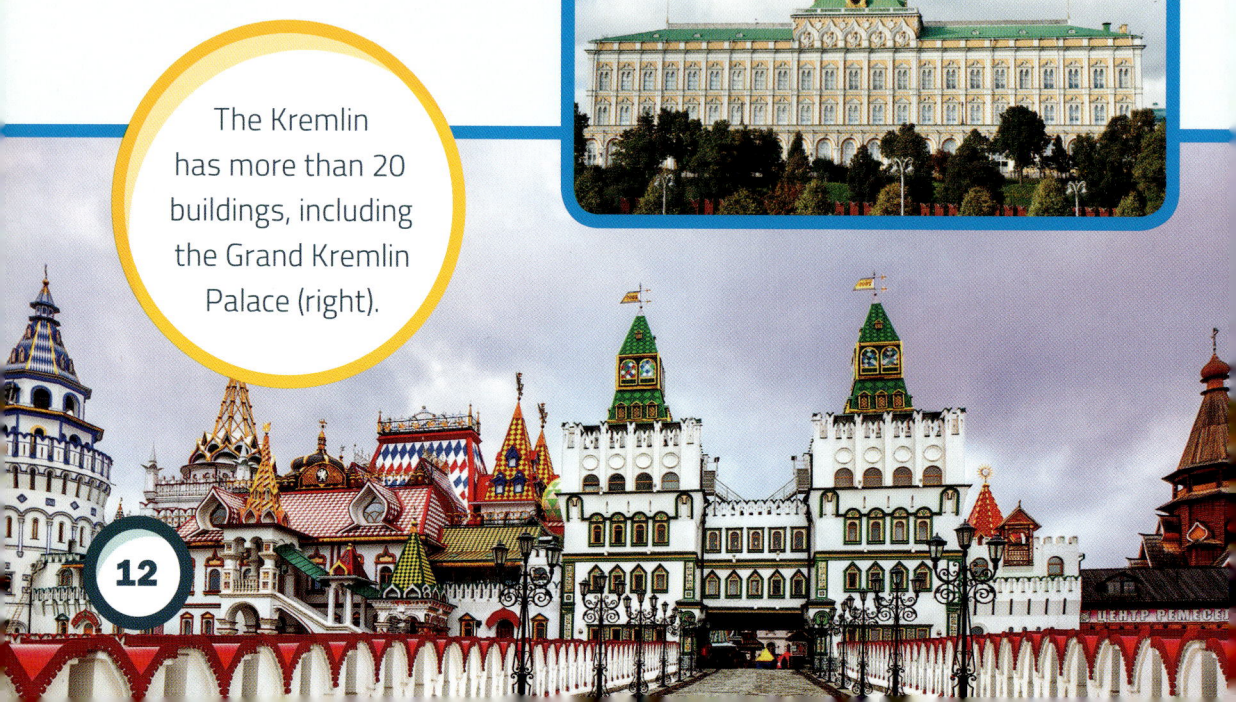

The Kremlin has more than 20 buildings, including the Grand Kremlin Palace (right).

70
Number of acres (28 hectares) the Kremlin covers

- The walls of the fort span more than 8,200 feet (2,500 m).
- The height of the walls ranges from 16 to 62 feet (5 to 19 m).
- The complex features 20 towers.

Plenty of Moscow's best-known buildings are centuries old. But the city also offers great modern architecture. The standout examples are in the west. Skyscrapers in Moscow rise high above the river. Evolution Tower and Federation Tower are two of Europe's largest structures.

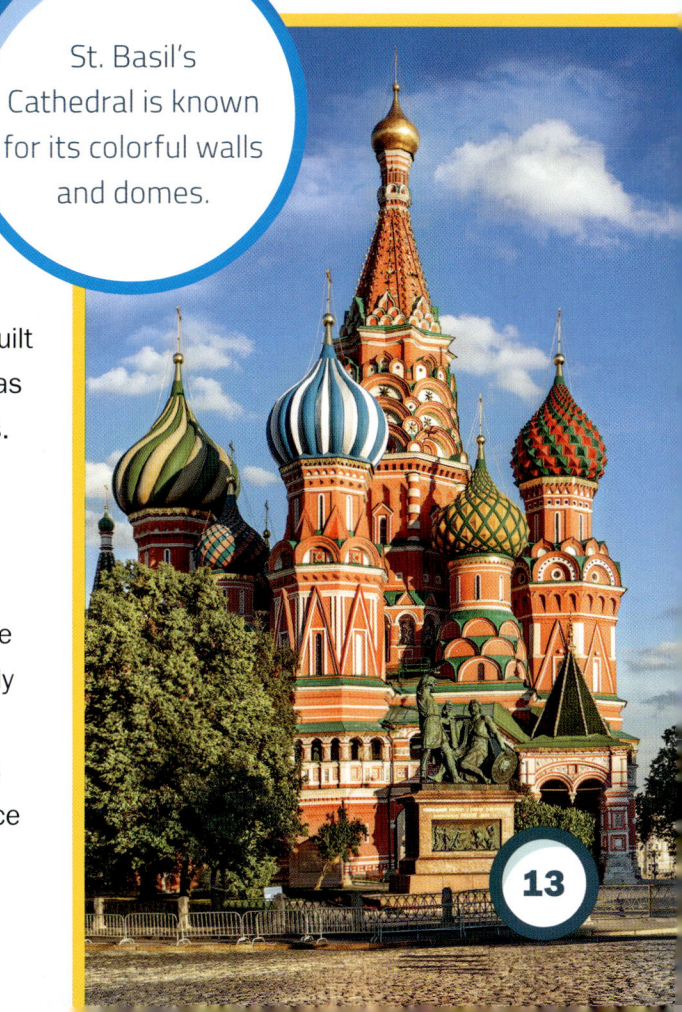

Tourists are dazzled by Moscow's cathedrals. The Assumption Cathedral, Archangel Cathedral, and Annunciation Cathedral were all built between 1475 and 1508. Each has white stone walls and gold domes.

Many other religious buildings feature famous architecture. St. Basil's Cathedral is built outside the Kremlin's walls. Finished in the sixteenth century, it has beautifully painted walls and domes. The church is set on Red Square. This has been an important public place in Moscow's history.

St. Basil's Cathedral is known for its colorful walls and domes.

6

Moscow's Infrastructure Is Vast and Crowded

Many people commute on the Moscow Metro. High-speed trains connect city neighborhoods and suburbs. Most routes are underground. The subway system is one of the largest in the world.

Railways extend outside the metro area. Routes connect Moscow with other cities in Russia. Many trains carry passengers. Others transport important cargo to and from Moscow businesses.

Another way people and goods reach Moscow is by water. The city is located on a major commercial waterway. The Moscow Canal allows large ships to dock at local terminals. This river

1935
Year when the Moscow Metro opened

- 13 stations served riders over 7 miles (11 km) of rails.
- Today the Moscow Metro has more than 200 stations.
- Up to 9 million riders take the subway every day.

14

traffic helps both the city and the national economy.

Back on land, people in Moscow increasingly own cars. The city's traffic jams are the worst in the world. Muscovites spend an average of 210 hours a year waiting in traffic. To ease congestion, more than 1,200 miles (1,900 km) of new and improved roads are planned.

People worry about the city's water safety. Decades of industrialization have polluted the Moscow River. Drinking water from the river is treated. But many are concerned that remaining toxic substances could cause health problems.

Moscow is known for its heavy traffic.

CENSORED

Most Muscovites can connect to the internet. People there have greater access than most others in Russia. But that does not mean they have full access. The Russian authorities block certain websites and communication apps. Laws require social media platforms to connect users' accounts with their phone numbers. This makes it hard for people to be anonymous. Security officials have access to users' online communications. People have demonstrated and protested.

15

7

The City Is a Center for Russia's Arts Scene

Russia's capital is the heart of the nation's culture. Moscow has 70 theaters and many concert halls. Most famous is the Bolshoi Theatre. Its history goes back more than 200 years. Visitors enjoy opera and ballet performances. Some take guided tours of the Bolshoi's grand halls.

Other Moscow sites focus on the visual arts. The Tretyakov Gallery has 17,000 works. Visitors learn how Russian art has changed over centuries. The site also hosts international exhibitions.

Two major museums focus on history. The Pushkin Museum has artifacts from civilizations going back centuries. The State Historical Museum is Russia's largest national museum. It houses millions of objects covering Russia's history from the Stone Age through the present day.

The Multimedia Art Museum presents modern works. It features photography and design exhibits. The Schusev State Museum of Architecture celebrates Russian buildings. Visitors

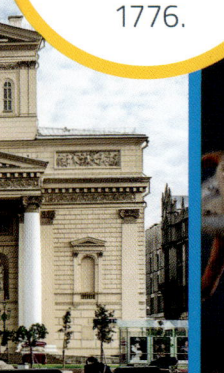

The Bolshoi Ballet was founded in 1776.

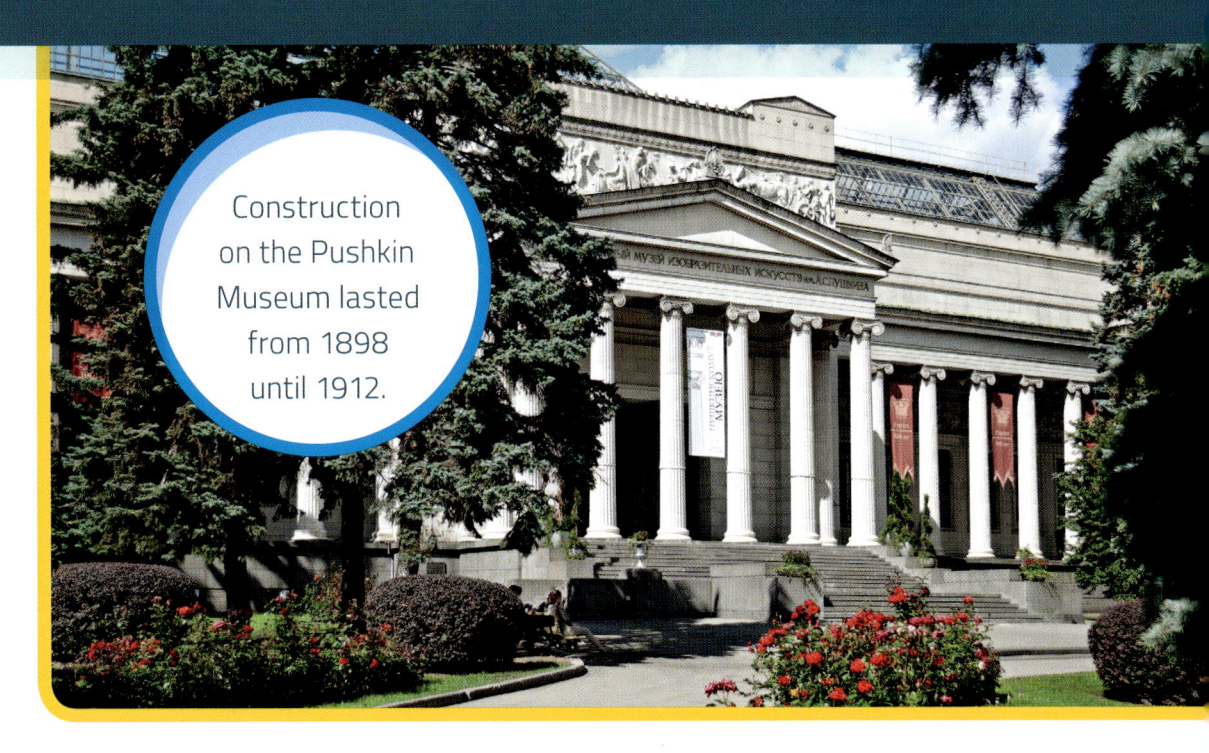

Construction on the Pushkin Museum lasted from 1898 until 1912.

can learn about famous structures in Moscow. Winzavod, a former brewery and wine plant, houses several galleries showing and selling contemporary art.

LITERARY MOSCOW

Moscow has a rich literary history. The poet Alexander Pushkin was born there in 1799. He is called the founder of modern Russian literature. Fyodor Dostoevsky was also born in Moscow. His family's nineteenth century apartment is now a museum. Nikolai Gogol is another famous writer. Visitors to the Gogol Museum can see where he created some of his most important works.

4.5 million
Number of items in Moscow's State Historical Museum

- The building stands on Red Square in the city center.
- Its two floors have 35 exhibit halls.
- The museum opened in 1883 during the coronation of Tsar Alexander III.

17

8

Sports Are a Big Part of Moscow Life

Muscovites take their sports very seriously. Some participate in athletics. Others turn out in crowds to support their favorite local and national teams. Moscow has many large stadiums. Fans of different teams fill the seats to cheer them on.

Football, or soccer, is among the most popular sports. Several football clubs play in Moscow.

People follow teams from their neighborhoods. Fans also show up to support Russia's national team. These footballers compete in international competitions.

Another loved sport is ice hockey. Moscow teams compete in the Kontinental Hockey League. Main rivals are from other Russian cities. Foes from Finland, Belarus, and other nearby nations also compete.

Fans support their Spartak football team.

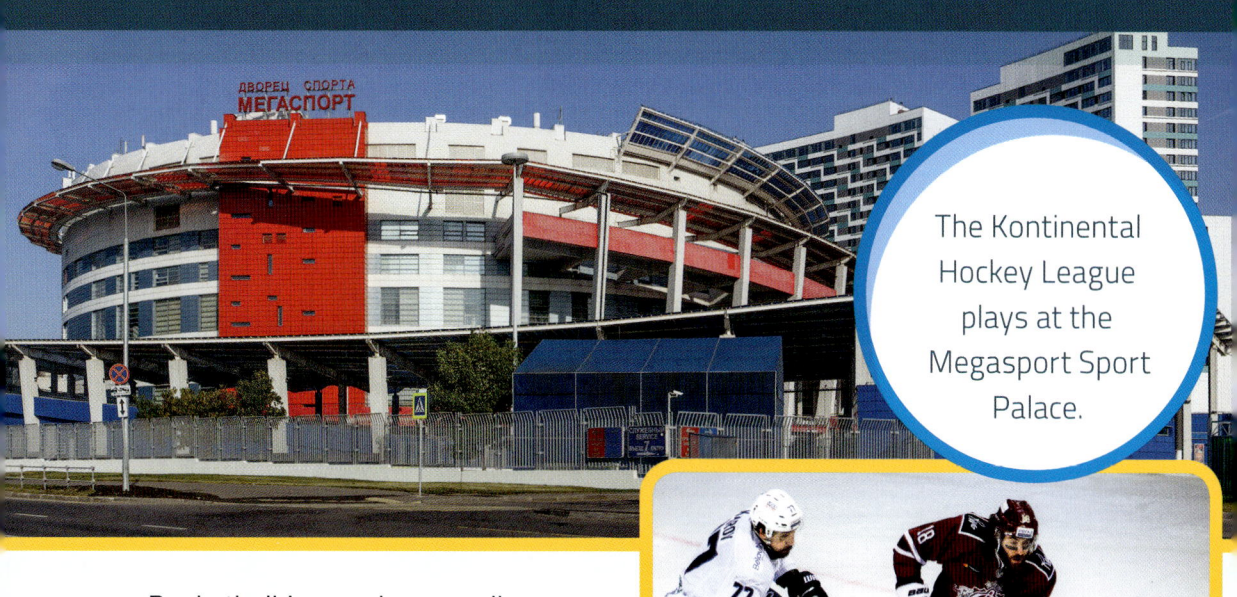

The Kontinental Hockey League plays at the Megasport Sport Palace.

Basketball is popular as well. Moscow's main professional team plays in the EuroLeague. CSKA Moscow has won multiple league titles against European competitors. The club plays its home games in Moscow's Megasport Sport Palace.

Individual sports are also very popular. Many Muscovites enjoy tennis, figure skating, and gymnastics. Children often begin these sports at a young age. Some athletes go on to achieve success at the international level.

There is no greater stage than the Olympics. Athletes from Moscow regularly compete in the Summer and Winter Games. Russia ranks among the top performing nations in the world.

1980
Year when Moscow hosted the Summer Olympics and the United States boycotted them

- The United States did not send athletes to Moscow because the Soviets invaded Afghanistan in 1979.
- Other nations also refused to participate.
- The total of 80 participating countries was the lowest since 1956.

19

9
Dramatic Views and Urban Adventures

A walk along the Moscow River offers great views. The Kremlin sits on its northern bank. The gold domes of the Annunciation Cathedral dominate the skyline. The Assumption Cathedral and Archangel Cathedral also rise up along the water.

Outside the Kremlin's east wall is Red Square. It has been a center of Russia's history for centuries. Political speeches and military parades have taken place there. So have protests and riots. It is known for public expression. Red Square markets draw locals and visitors alike.

Gorky Park is another popular spot. People relax in this leafy urban area. Cafés offer

The Victory Day Parade in Red Square commemorates the anniversary of the surrender of Nazi Germany in 1945.

Old Arbat Street is a popular destination for Moscovites.

casual dining. Free dance and yoga classes are provided. At night, an outdoor cinema entertains visitors.

Near Gorky Park is another site with green spaces. Moscow State University is built upon the Sparrow Hills. The city's highest area is just south of the Moscow River. The university's main building rises up more than 30 stories. It is the tallest educational building in the world.

800,000
Area in square feet (74,322 sq m) of Red Square

- The square was built more than 500 years ago.
- A moat once separated the square from the Kremlin.
- The moat was paved over in 1812.

OLD ARBAT STREET

Many visitors to Moscow go to Old Arbat Street. Restaurants, shops, and museums line this walkway through the city center. Families enjoy amusement rides and a petting zoo. The atmosphere is festive with many musicians playing on the street. Souvenir shops allow visitors to take home some memories of Moscow.

10
A Destination City for Food and Shopping

> Blini is often served with salmon and caviar.

Moscow is a center for Russian cuisine. The city has about 12,000 restaurants. They offer traditional Russian dishes and modern delights.

Dumplings are served throughout Moscow. Ingredients are enclosed in a dough shell. Fillings include pork, beef, fish, and lamb. Dumplings have diverse flavors. Some dishes are mild. Others can be very spicy.

Blini are another traditional Russian favorite. These are thin pancakes. Some are baked. Others are fried. Blini can be enjoyed in all kinds of ways. Breakfast options include butter and salmon. Diners may choose caviar or other toppings later in the day.

Famous restaurants are found throughout Moscow. Uhvat, Oblomov, and Severyane are a few. Each has traditional dishes as well as new twists on Russian food. StrEAT offers a different experience. More than 30 vendors serve unique bites at affordable prices.

Moscow also has high-end and bargain options for shopping. The GUM mall is set on Red Square. It is known for wealthy shoppers. Many global brands have stores in the mall. Locals and tourists shop for trendy clothes and goods.

THINK ABOUT IT

What foods are popular where you live? Are some similar to favorites in Moscow? How are eating experiences in your town or city different?

Other shops are more affordable. Moscow has many street markets. They are found in central shopping districts as well as the city's outer rings.

60,000
Number of daily visitors to the GUM mall

- Offerings include clothes, shoes, jewelry, cosmetics, and other goods.
- More than 2,000 employees serve customers.
- The mall is known for its architecture and a famous fountain.

The Moscow GUM mall was built between 1890 and 1893.

11

Wealthy and Poor Live Differently

Moscow is home to some very wealthy people. Most live in the city center. They enjoy fancy shopping and dining. Some rich families also own country properties. Often these are second homes used only in the summer.

A large majority of people experience working-class lives. Many cannot afford to live in the city center. Workers commute to their jobs from Moscow suburbs. They often live in high-rise apartments. Most families live in modest dwellings of a few rooms.

Suburban commuters who drive sit in terrible traffic. Others take the Moscow Metro. But stations can be far apart and hard to get to. Trains are frequently overcrowded. It often takes workers more than an hour to get to work.

Children in Moscow go to school for at least 11 years. This includes primary and

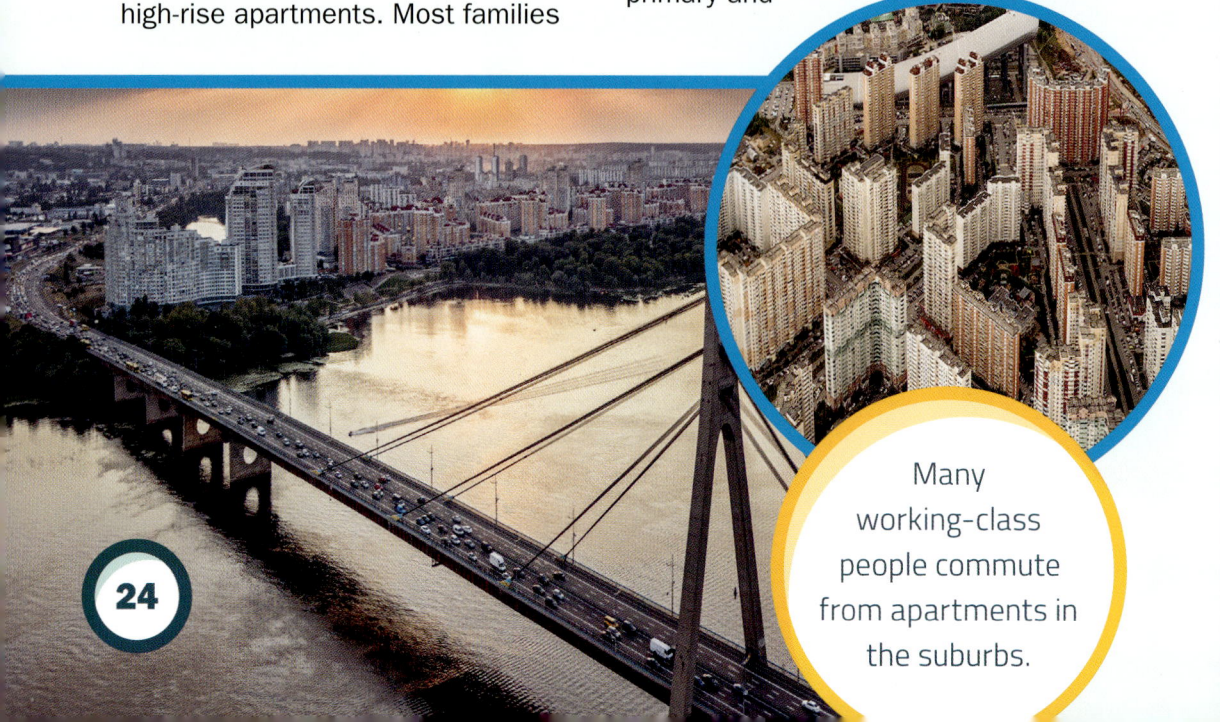

Many working-class people commute from apartments in the suburbs.

> Moscow State University was founded in 1755.

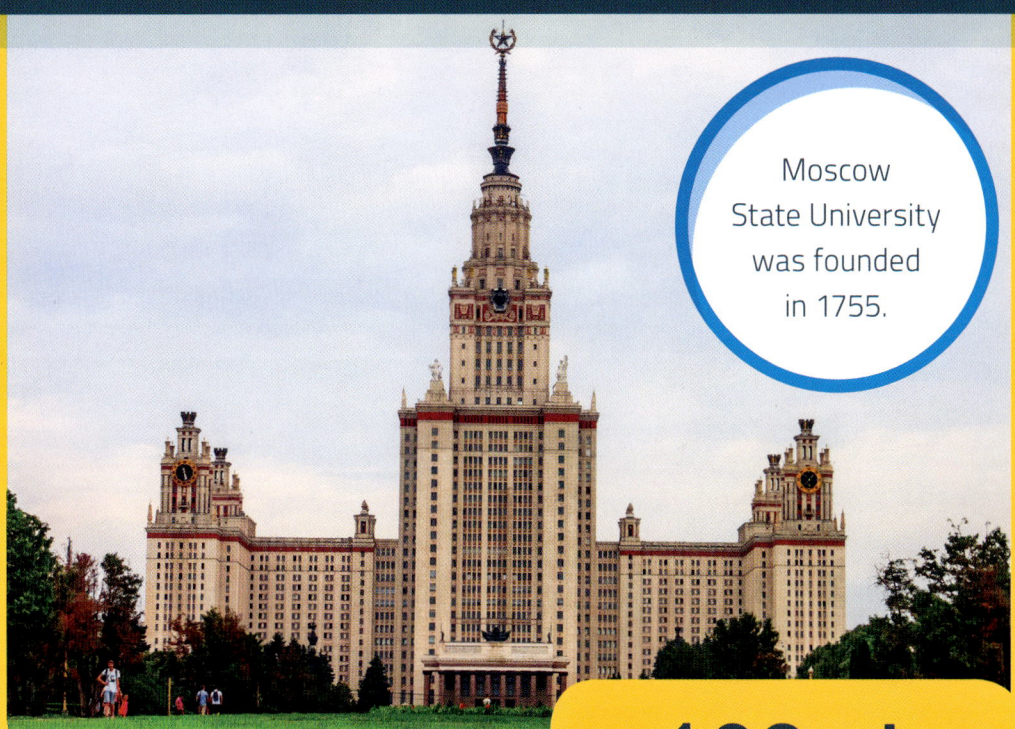

secondary school. Some students pursue higher education. The city universities are some of Russia's best. Moscow State University and the Moscow Institute of Physics and Technology rank high among world institutions.

102nd
Moscow's place on the 2019 list of the world's most expensive cities to live

- Singapore, Paris, and Hong Kong are tied for first place.
- Moscow is Russia's most expensive city, but many international cities are costlier.
- Many Muscovites struggle to pay for the essentials they need to survive. Migrant workers are among the city's poorest people.

THINK ABOUT IT
Is there a large gap in wealth where you live? Are some people super-rich? Are others very poor? What could be done to make things more equal?

12 Moscow Knows How to Celebrate

The New Year holiday is a Moscow favorite. Many workers have several days off. Some celebrate at home. Others go to concerts and dinners. Most Christians observe the Christmas holiday at this time.

Other holidays celebrate Russia. Defender of the Fatherland Day occurs in February. People enjoy concerts and fireworks. Victory Day marks the defeat of the Nazis in World War II. A Red Square parade is held in May. Russia Day, the nation's birthday, is June 12. This is a good reason for fireworks displays.

Summer offers fun. The Usadba Jazz Festival brings out music lovers. They listen to jazz, funk, blues, and world music on the lawns of an old estate. It is a famously laid-back festival. Park Live offers a different experience. This rock festival in Gorky Park hosts performances by major international artists. The Afisha Picnic is another event that draws fans. This one-day festival takes place on 1,000 acres (405 hectares) that used to be a tsar's estate.

People have many chances to celebrate Moscow's food. At the Taste of Moscow, dozens of local

8
Number of federal holidays in Russia each year

- Some people celebrate the New Year on both January 1 and January 14.
- The second celebration is the first day of the Julian calendar, once used in Russia.
- Diverse groups hold other festivals within their communities.

SPORTS EVENTS FEEL LIKE FESTIVALS

Large crowds flock to Moscow stadiums. Championships in football (soccer), ice hockey, and basketball are popular. Events have the feel of festivals. The game is only part of the fun. Russian national team contests bring the biggest crowds. Games are often shown on large screens. These outdoor watch parties are popular events.

chefs prepare dishes for the public. Tasty Moscow is another event. Chefs here prepare foods that were popular in Russia a century ago.

Gorky Park has many festivals and events.

Fun Facts about Moscow

- Area: 970 square miles (2,511 sq km). Population in 2019: 12.2 million.

- The Kremlin's walls were once made of white stone. Later construction produced the red walls we see today.

- Moscow has an underground river. The Neglinnaya flows almost 5 miles (7.5 km) through the central part of the city.

- People in Moscow eat 33,000 tons (29,937 metric tons) of food each day.

- Muscovites spend 773,650,800 rubles ($12 million) a day to fuel their cars.

- McDonald's opened its first Russian location in Moscow in 1990. More than 30,000 people were served in a single day—a record number.

- Moscow's subway system is the busiest in Europe.

- A law states that dogs in the city may not bark between 11 p.m. and 7 a.m.

Where in the World?

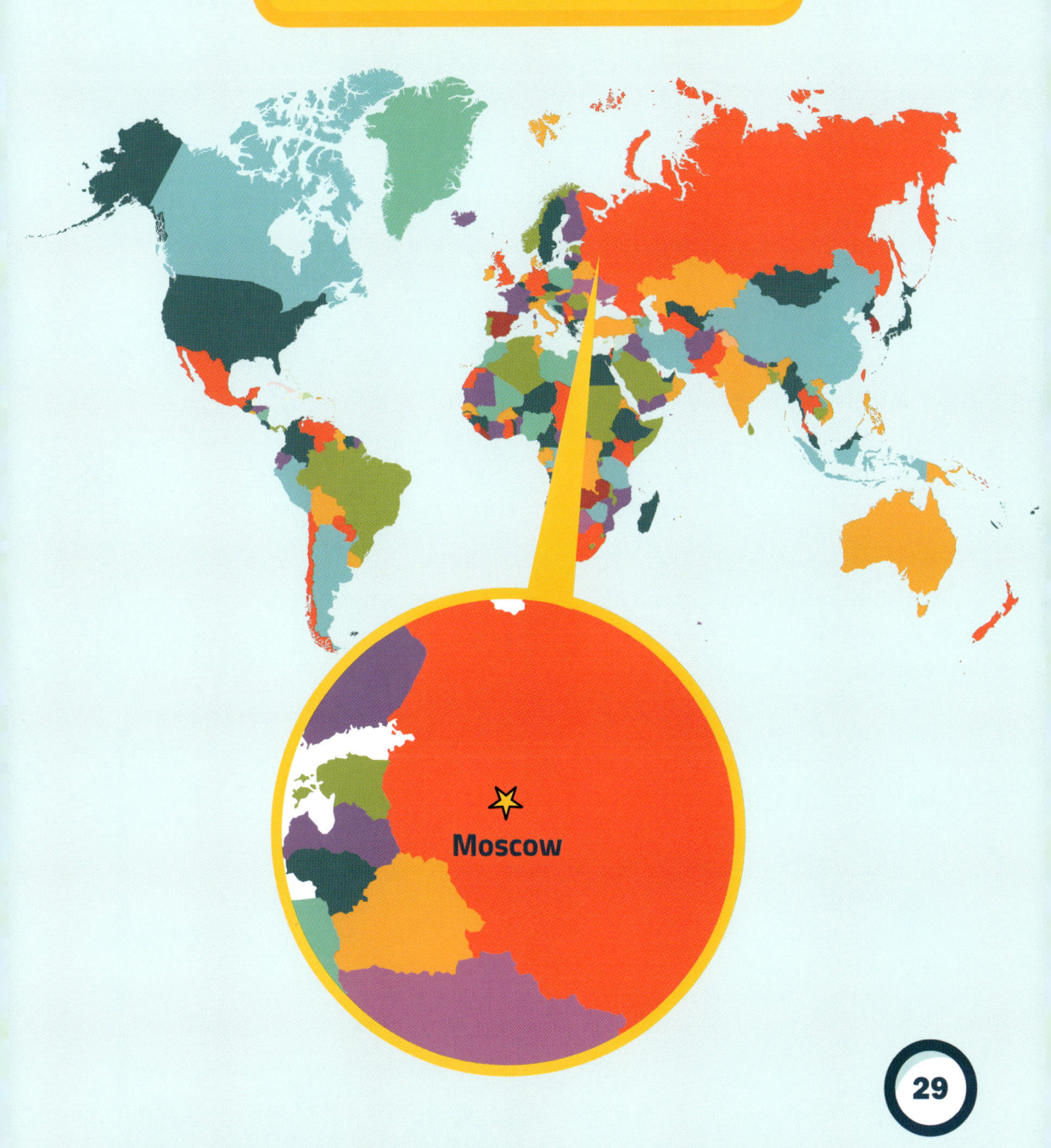

Moscow

Glossary

artifact
An object of historical or cultural importance.

censor
To remove some parts of an information source.

communism
A system in which the community, not individuals, owns property and goods.

coronation
A ceremony in which a nation's leader is crowned.

estate
Large property owned by one person or family.

industrialization
Widespread development of industries within a city or region.

precipitation
Rain, sleet, snow, and hail.

terminal
A place where people get on and off transit and goods are unloaded.

tsar
The title of Russia's leader before the Russian Revolution.

white-collar jobs
Positions in which most duties take place within an office.

Read More

DK Travel. *DK Eyewitness Travel: Moscow.* New York: DK Publishing, 2015.

Roman, Carole. *If You Were Me and Lived in … Russia: A Child's Introduction to Cultures around the World.* Andover, MA: Chelsea Inc., 2017.

Vorhees, Mara, and Leonid Ragozin. *Moscow.* London, UK: Lonely Planet, 2018.

Visit 12StoryLibrary.com

Scan the code or use your school's login at **12StoryLibrary.com** for recent updates about this topic and a full digital version of this book. Enjoy free access to:

- Digital ebook
- Breaking news updates
- Live content feeds
- Videos, interactive maps, and graphics
- Additional web resources

Note to educators: Visit 12StoryLibrary.com/register to sign up for free premium website access. Enjoy live content plus a full digital version of every 12-Story Library book you own for every student at your school.

Index

architecture, 12-13, 16, 23
arts, 16-17

daily life, 24-25

economy, 10-11, 15
education, 9, 21, 24-25

festivals, 26-27

government, 7, 10-11, 12

history, 6-7, 12-13, 16-17
housing, 24

internet access, 15

jobs, 10-11

Kremlin, 12-13, 20-21, 28

landscape, 4-5

Moscow River, 4-5, 15, 20

museums, 16-17

Olympics, 19

pay gap, 8, 11, 24-25
popular food, 22

popular sites, 12-13, 16-17, 20-21, 23
population, 8-9, 28

Red Square, 13, 20-21, 22
religion, 8-9

shopping districts, 22-23
sports, 18-19, 27

traffic congestion, 4, 15, 24
transportation, 14-15

weather, 5
writers, famous, 17

About the Author
Douglas J. Fehlen is an elementary educator. He is also a longtime editor of books for kids and teens. Douglas lives in Minnesota with his wife, their two dutiful dogs, and one mischievous cat.

READ MORE FROM 12-STORY LIBRARY

Every 12-Story Library Book is available in many fomats. For more information, visit 12StoryLibrary.com